Observations of Life in Verse

VIOLET HARRINGTON

Observations of Life in Verse

© 2024 Violet Harrington

Published by Texianer Verlag

Tuningen Germany

www.texianer.com

ISBN: 978-3-910667-12-9

All rights reserved

Contents

About Violet Harrington	7
That's me!	10
Someone Special	11
No Guarantee	12
Our beloved 'Chang'	13
The Mistress	14
It's Elvis!	15
It is too late!	16
What is it all about?	17
My young love	18
Maturity?	19
David and Jennifer	20
For the parents of Paul	21
It's Only Mum	22
Depression	23
Get Out Now!	24
For My Daughter	25
Just Say Hello!	26
Wasted	27

My Gold Coast	28
For my darling	29
Alive Again!	30
Be Honest	31
To go or stay	32
For David	33
Who's Kidding Who?	34
My Son	35
The time has come	36
None so Blind!	37
Homesickness	38
Understanding	39
No Wiser	40
Always Here For You!	41
At last	42
Crying	43
For Marie	44
The Book	45
A Loving Love	46
For my Cy	47
Adam and Eve	48

I know him so well	49
My Yorkshire Lass	50
It happens!	51
The Temptress	52
That special day	53
The Fortress	54
Facing up to it	55
My Wish	56
Christmas (with apologies)	57
The Bride	58
The Committed	59
And so it goes on	60
Condolences	61
Control	62
Old Age is not for Cowards	63
Hooked!	64
Let them go	65
Only words	66
My Daffodils	67
Candles	68
Don't complain!	69

Free Again!	70
Believe	71
You never know	72
For Miriam's Eighteenth Birthday	73
Joyous!	74
The Play	75
Save Something	76
Thanks Dear Mum	77
Conditioned?	78
I did my best	79
Please don't shout	80
Lizzie and Manfred 1974	81
I am so sorry!	82
Tell me now	83
My Granddad	84
Friendship	85
Tolerance	86
Please Go	87
Togetherness	88
Rock n' Roll	89

About Violet Harrington

Violet Harrington (Lorraine Roxon Harrington) was born in London, England in 1927. By nineteen she was a Lucy Clayton trained mannequin modelling in many of London's top fashion houses. In 1949 she married a doctor who later became a consultant psychiatrist. With him she had a daughter and two sons and is grandmother to nine grandchildren. She was involved in charity fund-raising for many causes and was Cultural Chairperson and President of a women's lodge in Bradford, W. Yorkshire.

In 1979 she left England and with her second husband moved to Auckland, New Zealand. Together they introduced the first sun tanning clinic to New Zealand. This led to the addition of beauty salons and Violet's own Beauty Therapy Training College. Violet became involved in publicity and advertising and was invited by the editor to write her own regular page on beauty in The NZ Headway Magazine. In 1987 she and her husband retired to Australia, making the Gold Coast their home and becoming Australian citizens. This gave Violet the freedom to satisfy her creative desires as an artist. Violet's interests are wide and varied and with the encouragement of her late husband, who sadly died in March 2000, she has been able to fulfil much of this creative potential. She is now a published writer, ceramicist, sculptor, and artist. Her original styled ceramics and paintings are in homes in many countries and one of her pieces of sculpture was exhibited at the Gold Coast Art Centre. Her artwork was selected from eighty-two entrants to be part of the Six Women Artists exhibition held at the Albert Shire Five Rivers Gallery in 1997. Violet has been writing for many years.

Her poetry has been broadcast on air in New Zealand and more recently, Somerset, England while her writings have been enjoyed far and wide. With the enthusiasm and encouragement of her late husband, family and friends, a collection of her verses has been now appended to her autobiography. Violet's style of poetry appeals in particular to the mature woman who is able to relate to much of its content.

That's me!

I expected to get old one day
With wrinkles and grey hair
I saw old people around me
Being young I did not care.
Now I'm old I know there's more
Than wrinkles and grey hair

Shoes become too heavy
Low chairs are out of bounds
Large printed text so I can read
Hearing aids so I hear sounds.
My lips appear much thinner
Bruised skin, I know not how
My eyes appear much dimmer
And my memory lets me down.
Shopping now becomes a chore
Too soon I want to get back home
Sit in the comfort of my chair
Feet up, relax and be alone.
No more outings of a night
Friends meet for lunches in the day
The afternoon is to rest and doze
Old folk find it best this way.
Pace is slower with painful joints
Knotted knuckles hard to hide
Life is not as it used to be
Old age is not so kind.

But then old age is a part of life
And for some it is a gift
Many have been robbed of this
And would gladly accept life as it is.
So I will think of those no longer here
And be thankful for what I've been given
And I will try to believe as many do
There's a wonderful place called Heaven

Someone Special

Has it all gone, can it be
The caring you once had for me?
For care you did, that much I know
Times we shared told me so.

They'll live on in my memory;
I gave to you, you gave to me
Shared a bond and sympathy
A happy laugh a gentle smile
Lit each others hearts a while.

It may be gone for you, dear friend
How I feel will never end
There will be others, that is true
But none will mean as much as you.

No Guarantee

I awake and I see
The dawn of a new day
Will I be at the end
Who can say?

This moment live
Not plan ahead
No thought of three score years
and ten.

Born that much I know
The moment passed I saw
Only God knows
If there's more.

Our beloved 'Chang'

ANIMAL LOVERS WILL UNDERSTAND.

We knew that there would come a day
When our lovely Chang would go
We knew that we would suffer
Because we loved him so.
His gentle look that said so much
His walk, the way he lay
Everything about him
Gave us pleasure every day.
Sadly he has slipped away
And with pain so hard to bear
Our days are now so empty
With our Chang no longer there.
We loved him, truly loved him
He was our pal our trusted friend
And now we face each day ahead
With hearts that will not mend.
Friends tell us time will heal our loss
We know this must be true
But time is going much too slow
And there is nothing we can do.
"Get another dog" they say
"Fill your hearts again
It will help you to forget
And is sure to ease your pain".
Replace our Chang so easily
This we cannot do
We would feel disloyal
To our friend who was so true.
We know we have to carry on
And in time our hearts will mend
But the memory will last forever
Of Chang, our pal, our friend.

The Mistress

A warm and caring friendship
That's all that it can be
The man he loves another
But the woman, she is free.

Free to give and fulfil the need
That lies within this man
Although she knows it will not last
She enjoys him while she can.

She gives he takes what's offered
This is his way of life
Momentary joy with others
When his real need is his wife.

If his wife would only realize
If she could only see
That whilst he's with another
He's wishing it were she

If you're a wife look closely
See yourself and don't blame me
If you could love him as you did before
He would have no need of me.

It's Elvis!

I know that you all love me
And feel I'm still around
That one day, some place, somehow,
I'll turn up safe and sound.
The trusty Rock n' Rollers
Make sure I'll never die
I watch them swing and sing along
From up here in the sky.
My Graceland's now a shrine
I see Folk come from far and wide
They give respect and honour me
I feel I want to cry.
I'd like to let my fans all know
I'm still around and singing
Guitar playing loud and clear
My hips are still a'swinging.
In heaven here with many friends
We really have a ball
They sing together
'Long live the King
The greatest of them all.'
I left, it was not easy,
I did not want to go; but
Friends up here were calling me,
I was needed in the show.
Thank you all for loving me
I am happy and feel proud,
Just keep on looking,
You never know,
You might see me in the crowd.

It is too late!

I said 'Goodbye' it has to be
I have ties I must respect
I am not free to give to you
The loving you expect.

Doing what I know is right
Relieves some of my pain
Now you phone me as before
Saying we must meet again.

Help me please I have to keep
The decision that I made,
I cannot suffer the guilt I feel
I cannot face the shame.

Respect the love I feel for you
Allow it time to go,
This is the way it has to be
Please stay away!
Please go!

**THIS POEM WAS WRITTEN AFTER
THE NEWS OF TERRORIST BOMBINGS**

What is it all about?

War is war and people die
No preference is shown
Old or young woman or child
Men dead and broken homes.

Fighting for a chosen cause
May make it seem alright
People die and people cry
Can the cause be ever right?

Bringing suffering and causing pain
Never seems to end
Wars are won and lives are lost
And then it starts again.

Who is right, who is wrong
One never gets to know
Enemies later become our friends
And we let the anger go.

Older and much wiser now
I accept the way it will always be
Religious beliefs will divide us all
Making enemies we never see.

My young love

He's young my love
And says he cannot see
That I am slowly changing
And age is creeping up on me

I won't question if his love is true
I doubt if he can say
I'll close my ears to my kindly friends
And what they have to say.

I'll be brave and take a chance
I'll accept there could be pain
Though short may be the happiness
It's good to feel in love again.

Maturity?

This man I need, needs me
Both of us aware
Neither look for permanence
Although we know we care.

Both are free to say "Goodbye"
When our need has gone
Sensible and logical
Accepting that we care
Never giving time the chance
To spoil that which we share

Each giving to each other
Taking as we give
Grateful for this chance that came
Happy so to live.

David and Jennifer

BY SPECIAL REQUEST
Today we have witnessed a wedding
The joining of two people in love
Vows have been made before us all
With blessings from up above.

Marriage is not always easy
It needs commitment to survive
Lots of love, respect and laughter
Helps a marriage stay alive.

Jenny and David have been together
Have had time to find the key
That opens the door to happiness
And lets love shine from within.

Knowing this couple as we do
We are certain their future will flourish
For they possess those essential qualities
Of loyalty, of love and of courage.

Commitment has now been taken
Together they start a new life
David is Jennifer's husband
And Jennifer is now David's wife.

We give our love to both of them
And we could go on about them all day
But we will leave it now to their families
Who will say all we want to say.

For the parents of Paul

Our son was born our son was lost,
If only he could see
Bent on his own destruction
No thought for you or me.
We say he is at peace now
But questions will remain
We gave him all that we could give
Alas it was in vain.

A kind of peace his dying brought
As years of pain he gave
We prayed he'd have a future
Himself he chose his grave.
Did we go wrong did we fail,
This son we loved so well
Does someone know the answer
Is it possible to tell?

The trauma of those dreadful years
The suffering and the pain
Made us lose the love we shared
It will not return again.
We pile up all the sadness
The blame and all the guilt
A wall of stone divides us now
A wall we both have built.

Our son was here and now he's gone
If he could only see
While drugs killed only one of us
It took the lives of three.

It's Only Mum

I gave my all when they were small
And now that they have grown
I felt it right to have some time
Time just for me alone.

My children knew I loved them
I was there when they needed me
Knowing this they used me well
Thinking always of themselves
With little thought for me.

The time had come to say enough
It's time I had some life
Time for me to look around
And see what I'd been missing
Maybe get something back
Instead of always giving.

Now I find to my surprise
Because I am thinking of me
The children think I am selfish
And not happy with what they see.

I have to laugh it's quite a joke
To find now I've grown old
They think that I should baby sit
And do as I am told.

Depression

FOR MY FRIEND LUCY

The depth of sadness that I feel no one can ever know
I try so hard to hide it and hope it does not show.
I drag my feet and every step I hope will be the last
Tears come quickly to my eyes I try to dry them fast.

'There are others worse than you' so many times I say
Though aware, it doesn't help it does not ease this pain.
Is my life worth living, does it mean so much?
Do I have to suffer so when I have had enough?

Despair, depressed and lonely the pain is always there.
I do have friends who help me and a family who care.
I take the pills they help at times the doctor said they may
Too soon the black clouds hover and I'm depressed again.

It is hard for those around me they never know my mood
One moment happy and then I'm sad
They don't know what to do.
All I can do is pray and hope and I do this every day
It is sad to suffer with depression
It's so hard to live this way.

Lucy was twelve and an only child of Jewish parents. She was one of the many children who were put on trains and left Vienna to live in England where they would be safe from the Nazis.

Lucy never knew what happened to her father; she never saw him again. She found her mother through The Red Cross when the war ended. Her mother had managed to get to Israel after being in a concentration camp. Her mother died soon after Lucy found her. Lucy was highly intelligent and held the position of Draughtswoman at the local Council. She had a child, a daughter, who became a nurse and married a doctor. Sadly Lucy died of cancer, aged 60 without seeing her daughter married.

Get Out Now!

The way you choose
To live your life
Is yours alone you say
No one else's business
If you choose to live this way

No one else's business?
Do you ever give a thought
To the ones who gave you life
And a future that they sought.

The caring and the loving
Through all those childish ills
Now heartache pain and misery
You thoughtlessly instil.

Get out now while there is time
We know it is hard to do
Your life is not yours alone
Others are part of it too.

They do not want to own you
They want you to live free
But they know as you do too
With drugs this will never be.

For My Daughter

Daughter dear daughter,
What did I do?
I gave you a picture
Which was untrue.

When you were a child
I let you believe
That a man could be loved
When he'd no right to be.

A woman downtrodden
No respect as a wife,
Quarrels, injustice,
The fear and the strife.

Seeing it all
I know caused you pain,
Never quite knowing,
Which parent to blame.

The fact that I stayed
I know now was wrong,
But love for my children,
Made me be strong,

Scars still remain
And memories will last,
But don't let your future
Be ruled by my past.

Just Say Hello!

Ready to go and leave this world,
Old folk sometimes feel this way
Had enough, done my share
You may hear them say.
The world is not the same they say
Nothing is like it was
No one cares as they used to do
No one loves enough.
Years ago, daughters and sons
Brothers and sisters, lived nearby
Scattered now around the world
They do not hear the cry.
Crying for the days gone by when
Children played, and families gathered
Meals shared at the table
Discussing events that really mattered.
Honour, respect, was part of life
Children knew the score
They were taught and shown the values
Of family life and more.
Duty was a part of life
It was not frowned upon
Family and friends were there to help
Now those days have gone
All alone most of the time,
Old friends have passed away
There is no one left to chat to,
No one comes to stay.
So if you hear "I've had enough"
Be kind and understand
Just give a little of your time
And hold out a friendly hand.

Wasted

She loved him well and tried so hard
So that he would know
Waited on him hand and foot
This way her love to show
Scrimped and saved, made a home
Bore him children three
Two sons and a daughter
A joy for all to see.
Position came and money too
A life of ease was there
But it was not this way to be
The man then did not share.
He clung to gold to jewellery,
Kept it locked away
Making life a misery
Not thinking of today,
It soon was an obsession
Of meanness and of greed
Never thinking he could lose
Material wealth his need.
And so he lost the wife who once
Loved him far too well
She had enough, could take no more,
He'd made her life a hell.
Be wise and recognize true wealth
And place it high above
Or you could end up like this man
No wife, no home, no love.

My Gold Coast

As the sun spreads its morning glow,
And birds awake us with their singing,
'Kookies' laugh, as if they know
A great day is beginning.
We look at the picture, the green and the gold,
The blue of the ocean , the colours so bold,
Bright sunny skies, with beaches, so clean,
The Hinterland backdrop,
All luscious and green.
Places to go, new places to see,
A millionaire's lifestyle,
What more could you need?

There's always good fun happening here,
The pokies, the clubs, and the good Aussie beer.
The surfers, the swimmers, the Mums and the Dads
The kids, and the seniors, the girls and the lads
All sorts of people, holiday here,
Returning again, year after year.
We like to be helpful, do not want to seem mean,
Please when you arrive and look at the scene,
Walk through the forests, and the Hinterland green,
Swim in the ocean, with its beaches so clean,
Be kind and please leave them,
As they were when you came
It makes it much nicer,
When you visit again.

For my darling

You have gone
Out of my life
Forever
Will I forget you?
The answer is
Never
How could death
Be so unkind
Take you from me
And leave me
Behind.
To suffer this way
So that every day
Is so hard to live
Without you

Alive Again!

The humour is back,
The dramas have gone
It's true and it is so
But the pain I suffered
You will never know.

It's good to feel myself again
And know that I am free
No more waiting by the phone
Hoping you would ring.

The way I felt about you
Caused me too much pain
I'm glad that it's all over
And I'm myself again.

Be Honest

Love can be a burden
Married life a strain
Some will take it happily
Others will refrain.

There are those
Once love has gone
Continue with the farce
Accepting with indifference
Go on, no questions ask.

Others knowing what is left
See and face the fact
In so doing play no part
Withdraw and leave the act.

What others see, what others say
Can be a mockery
If when you look and see yourself
You don't like what you see.

Whichever way you live your life
Whatever way you choose
The most important thing of all
Is to thine own self be true.

To go or stay

A time to come
And a time to go
Watch the signs
Know what they say.

Look close enough
And you will see
A smile, the warmth,
A need to talk
A touch!
You're bound to know

So important when to stay
Much more when time to go.

For David

What can I do, what can I say?
I am tied so helplessly
I must not write I cannot phone
Your sadness is hurting me.

I want to take you in my arms
To comfort and ease your pain
I know how you are suffering
And I am so far away.

It's life, my love, and you will find
The strength to see it through
I know I cannot say the words
To make it easier for you

So my friend I read your words
They make me want to cry
I wish for you this Christmas Eve
An angel by your side.

If only God could spare one
To comfort you and guide
Lift up your heart a little
And help you through this time.

To pray is all that I can do
And in my simplicity
I am hoping God will listen
And will pity me.

Who's Kidding Who?

'Enjoy your life!' so many times
My love says this to me
Is he fooling himself
Or is he kidding me?
I'll be wise and play the game
I know he wants me to
I'll talk of everyday events
Ask what he's been doing too.

I will not mention how my life
Is empty without him
Won't say I count the hours
Until we meet again.
I'll keep it full of humour
Make it light and say
All the things he likes me to
I know it's best this way.

He doesn't want it heavy
Doesn't like to feel restrained
No ties, no pressure, no commitment
Just free to go his way.
I'll carry on the way we are
And play his silly game
I will not let it bother me
I know he's got to change.

Some day I know he'll realize
One day he's bound to see
Although he doesn't know it now
I know my love loves me.

My Son

I wonder if you realize
The love I feel for you
I am not allowed to show it
The way I used to do.

You are grown up now
You are a man
Of this I am aware
Although you try to hide it
I see the child still there.

Recently I've noticed
A situation which is new
You feel no longer you're a child
But I am a child to you.

There'll come a time in later years
And you will see my son
You will once more feel the child
And will see me as your Mum.

The time has come

I cannot go on it has to end
The way you are I cannot bear
You tell me that you love me
But you never show you care

Your selfishness is evident
Your demands on me unfair
I don't know why I bothered
But there was a time I cared.

My future is looking brighter
Now I know what I have to do
With no regrets I have to say
'Goodbye my love
We're through'.

None so Blind!

O.K. I thumped her
Well, so what!
The bruises soon will fade
She knows I have a temper
She knows the way I'm made.

She should watch how she reacts
When I am in a mood
Keep away and not answer back
I don't like it when she's rude.

Sometimes I might be in the wrong
Perhaps should say "I'm sorry"
But why should I? when she's the one
Who gives me all the worry?

I think the children get upset,
And are frightened by my tone
I notice they don't come to me
Whenever I'm at home.

Things will change, they have to!
I cannot go on with this life
I will wait and I will be patient
And hope for a change in my wife.

I know she will come to her senses
And I'm sure one day she will see
That she is the one with a problem
As there is nothing wrong with me.

Homesickness

WRITTEN FOR RICK!

Ears that do not hear
Eyes that do not see
Longing, sadness and despair
My daily company.
Far away from those I love
Lost, and all so much alone
Remembering how I used to be
I tell myself, this can't be me
And yet I see the 'Me' that was
There outside of me.
The hearty laugh the carefree mood
I play the clown and act the fool
And let no other see
The 'Me' inside of me.

But I was wrong, you came along
And recognised the scene
Remembering how you once were
You saw, the 'Me'… in me.

You took my hand, and called me friend
Helped me and got me through.
I will always remember
I will never forget
That wonderful person
Inside of you…

Understanding

The frown I see
Upon your face
Will slowly fade
As we embrace.

We will not talk,
No words we'll say
As I smooth
Your cares away
Lie with me

Stay in my arms
Just for a little while
And I will hold you
Close to me
Until I see you smile.

No Wiser

It's not the same is it?
Your letters they have changed
Not so many phone calls
It really is a shame.
It was lovely while it lasted
Now I know it's at an end
My fault, I know.
The rules I broke
I was too intense.

Now you could take it calmly
It was not new for you
But I was inexperienced
And knew not what to do.
Do not think I am complaining
It's been wonderful for me
I have loved and learned
Been taught a lot, now face reality.

Better equipped and able to cope
Next time my love I will withhold
I will not give my all again
I will not get so much involved.

What nonsense I am writing
I know I will never change
The same mistakes the heartache
It will happen all again.
Life for me is living
I give and I receive
Those times we spent together
Were worth it all for me.

Always Here For You!

I'm always here and giving
Whenever you need me
Lift you up, when you feel low
Never let my worries show
Always here and giving.

There are times when I feel down
No desire to play the clown
Time when I need you to share
Time for me to feel you care.

I look to you to ease my pain
And help me be myself again
The role reversed you cannot take
"Why are things not in their place?"

You scowl find fault make things worse
The children watch you shout and curse
You look at me not see the pain
"How long till you are well again?"

It's sad I know you cannot see
What your actions do to me
All the care that I like giving
Will one day fade, be spent
Then you will look around and wonder
Where all the giving went.

At last

We were young and we were happy
Made love, and felt as one
Made sure the bedroom door was locked
And kept our nightclothes on.

No sounds we'd make, always alert
In case the children called
Soon it became a ritual
Love played no part at all.

Slowly passion fades away
You wonder where it went.
Returning but not staying long,
You decide that it's all spent.

Years have passed and we are old
Our 'kids' have all left home.
Our passion has returned
Now we are on our own.

There is no rush we take our time
Make love, as once before.
Much better now we do not ask,
"Are you sure you locked the door"?

Crying

FOR MY GRANDSON GABRIEL

Don't cry now come dry those tears
You're a big boy now all three years
Big boys don't cry that's what we say
You should know better now go and play.

What do we do to babes of three
What do we make them out to be?
We shed our tears when we are old
We are not too young then to be told

But then we're told don't be a babe
Come dry your tears and act your age.
Why can't we cry be the way we feel
It helps our aching hearts to heal.

Gabriel was killed with three other students from Exeter College when he was almost eighteen after being involved in a car accident as a passenger.
At the time he was Vice President of the Students Union and had been involved in creating a crèche for the students with babies.
Some time after he died the College approached his parents and with their permission the crèche was named after him.

For Marie

He died my brave young husband
Lost, like others in the war
I knew not where his body lay
No one was left who saw.

I thought it was impossible
I could ever love again
But with time there came
A gentle man
Who offered me his name.

We married and lived happily
I loved as once before
We had many years of happiness
No one could ask for more.

We planned our lives together
Old age we hoped we'd see
But death then came
A second time
And took my man from me.

Now once more a widow
Full of grief and pain
Left to live my life alone
No love to give again.

So now I wait and pray each day
In all sincerity
That I won't have to wait too long
For death to call on me.

The Book

I knew that this would happen
I thought I'd be prepared
But it came so suddenly
No suffering was I spared.

I was brave you must agree
As we said "Goodbye"
"Yes I understand" I said
'No I will not cry".

The pain that lies within me now
I'll try hard not to show,
The way I act, the way I feel
No-one will ever know.

Life goes on as it will,
It's there, and must be lived
So I will go on as I can
And make the best of it.

Close the book and finish
Search and look ahead
Life is like a library
With books waiting to be read.

The book I read was special
It's story will remain,
Staying only in my memory
Never to be read again.

A Loving Love

Gentle, fond, caring and true
That is the way
I feel for you
A warmth
And loving tenderness
As my thoughts
Upon you rest.

There is a peace
That absence brought
A quality that time has taught
The seeds we planted
Now have grown
And a greater love I know.

Because you make me
Feel this way
I want to thank you
And I need to say
I know for sure
And believe it's true
The love you give
Makes me love you.

For my Cy

Stay with me please don't go
Do not leave me all alone

Stay with me in my memory
Be beside me when I walk
Answer me when I talk
Always stay beside me.

Stay with me until I die
Join me then and hold my hand
Guide my way so we can fly
As we did before
This time to stay together
For evermore.

Adam and Eve

Like babes they took each others hand
And walked down to the sea
A quiet, thoughtful lonely man
A woman alive and free..

No guilt, no questioning was there
No serpent to be seen
The apple, still unbitten
Remained upon the tree.

Both had passed their days of youth
They knew of lies, they knew of truth
But innocence was theirs that day
They played no games that others play.

And so dear God, I pray of thee,
Please let their joy stay always free
As on that day they first held hands
And walked down to the sea.

I know him so well

Let's face the truth, be honest
Let's call a spade a spade
I find it hard to believe
And I think it's all a charade.
The love you pretend you are feeling
I know it can't be true.
Each day I see you doing
Things people expect from you.
I know you must be feeling sad
And I accept this as a fact
But I have to question the role you play
As I see it as an act.
Socialising plays no part
When the one you love is dying
Planning to enjoy yourself
Must show that you are lying.
We like to kid ourselves and see,
Only the good that's in our hearts
We try to forget all the bad things
And remember the nicest parts.
So do your best and play the part
Pretend the way you do
It will be easier when the end comes
For her and so for you.
A part of you may suffer
I'm not sure if it will be
But don't overdo the mourning
It really won't wash with me.

My Yorkshire Lass

What a woman is our Madge
Generous to a fault
If there's a need she will give
And leave herself with naught.

Trouble comes, our Madge is there
She'll help to see you through
She may have troubles of her own
But first she'll see to you.

Sit and listen, have a chat
Clean the house right through
She will see what help is needed
And freely give it to you.

A lovely smile, a tender heart
But tough if need must be
Don't underestimate our Madge
There's a lot you do not see.

To Madge I dedicate these words
Your friends will echo them too
The world would be a better place
If more lasses were like you.

It happens!

A woman full of love to give
A man whose need was there
A special warm, and kindly man
Of this she was aware

Their bodies joined
That was not all
Could satisfy this pair
They had a trusting friendship
Not a common place affair.

But there is more to this she feels
And knows instinctively
The years will pass and he will know
What she already sees.

It is sad, he cannot give
His love so easily
Too much of life
Has made him feel
To love is slavery.

Give and feel just what you can
That's all she asks of you
For her to love came easily
One day maybe for you.

The Temptress

Long soft fingers
Hands, gently stroke
The body trembles
As emotions she invokes
Kisses, gentle sweet to taste
Each moment lived
Nothing waste
Searching hands,
The temptress

As her reward she finds
Bodies joined,
Legs entwined
A cry of joy
Then deep, a sigh
Pleasure shared
Though short the time.

That special day

Why did I choose you?
Why did you choose me?
Did we ever have a say
In what was meant to be?

It happened all so suddenly
I felt that we were lost
No thought, just joy,
The need to share
No time to count the cost.

Fate stepped in and took a hand
Everything seemed right
We two alone, the world was still
Not a bird in flight.

So in the book that is my life
One golden page will shine
Forever printed in my heart
That day when you were mine.

The Fortress

It was there,
I sensed it,
A barrier a wall
There for me
To push aside
Join you
Behind that wall.

No so! A fortress
Locked up tight
No heart to give
To need to
Shake the wall.

Remain apart
Locked inside
Keep your heart
Whilst others fall
Off the wall.

Bruised and sore
Arise and leave
You all alone
Just as you were before.

Facing up to it

So much to say,
So many things
Are happening to me
My love affair has ended
And once again I'm free;
Free to be the way I was
Before you came along
No more deceit, no one to hurt
No guilt for what went on.
I believed that what we did
No one would ever know
But now I face the truth and say
It's best that you should go.
I realized that it was wrong
And no future could there be
Though I loved you truly
This way is best for me.

My Wish

When I die, it is my wish
That my ashes should fly free
To join again with those I've loved
Who have gone before me.

I want no flowers bright and fresh
To accompany me
Knowing that within one week
Dead, like me they'll be.

No mournful black should be worn
But colours bright and gay
With friends and family looking good
To see me on my way.

So if you're around at this time
No sadness must there be
Cause if you're sad and miserable
You'll only upset me.

Christmas (with apologies)

Xmas comes but once a year
And we celebrate God's son
I spend and all my money goes
On Xmas gifts and fun.

Xmas comes and then it's gone
Now comes the hardest part
Paying off my credit cards
It really breaks my heart.

Xmas comes but once a year
And we celebrate God's son.
I'm glad God didn't have more kids,
It costs enough for one.

The Bride

Tightly she holds on to my arm
I hear the swish of silk and lace
This girl who walks beside me
Now has a woman's grace.

I see the congregation I look ahead and smile
Soon will come the moment when I give up my child
I turn and gaze upon her, she turns looks at my face
A special love she holds for me no one can take that place.

And as we walk so slowly there stands another bride
I see her as she was before when youth was on our side.
No longer young, still beautiful thirty years have passed
Our love has stood many tests we worked and made it last.

She looks at me and our eyes meet
So much is said, no need to speak
We've been there and we know the scene
Now it's our daughter's time to dream.

Both of us are full of love of happiness and sharing
Giving up our daughter to another's love and caring.
The music stops the church is still, the moment has arrived
She stands beside the man she loves a beautiful young bride.

We wipe our tears as their vows are said
And we think of our new life
And wonder how our lives will change
Now our daughter is a wife.

The Committed

The situation was so new
You spelt it out for me
Loving you might cause me pain
I listened carefully.

How wrong I was I paid no heed
To what you kindly said
Holding you and kissing
My heart ruled not my head.

Well here I am… I never thought
That time could pass so slow
That I would long for you so much
And I would miss you so!

So there it is, I don't complain
Was warned and told the score
But I would rather feel this way
That not know you at all.

And so it goes on

Decision forced upon me,
And I'm still very young
Should I stay with my Dad?
Should I go with Mum?
Live with Dad, leave Mum alone,
Live with Mum, what then?
Can't they wait a few more years,
Can't they try again?
They say it is impossible,
Divorce it has to be,
They think only of themselves
With little thought for me
So here am I it's left to me,
And whichever way I choose,
I know that I will suffer,
I know I'm bound to lose.

Years have passed I'm older
I have two children and a wife
I have to make a decision again
Which I know will change my life.
I understand my parents now
As no other way can I see
I have no choice but have to say
Divorce it is has to be.

Condolences

IN MEMORY OF JEAN 2ND MARCH 2009

I admired the way Jean managed her life
A good mother, a friend, a companion, a wife.
Her home always tidy, no dust to be seen
Always calm, and collected was my friend Jean.
The washing and ironing all nicely put away
The twins in their cots, Norm out to play
Her work was all done, her time to relax
A coffee, a cigarette, phone a friend,
Have a chat
I so much wanted to be like Jean
To be organised tidy and looking serene
But strange as it sounds
And it's hard to conceive
Jean told me she wanted to be like me.
I suppose with my gregarious ways
No plans, no routine, just live for today
Might have seemed attractive
To someone like Jean
Who always was organised tidy and clean
Though we have lived many miles apart
The bond that we shared was born in the past
She was part of my life and a part of me
My wonderful dearest and loving friend
Jean!

Control

I treat you well and let you be
The woman I want you to be.
I listen to you when I can
Although I am a busy man.
I buy you all the things I like
And when I take you out at night
I make a point so people see.
You have learned a lot from me.

And when you ask, I always say?
"I love you more and more each day."
Yet why is it with all I do you
You seem so sad, no longer 'you'?
You rarely laugh, and you hardly smile
I ask myself if it's all worth while?
But I will wait and patiently
By going on, just being me
And doing all I do for you.
You'll be again, the girl I knew.

Old Age is not for Cowards

I've reached the age of eighty three
And I never thought that it would be
They say you're old as you feel
But is that good if you're feeling ill.

You are told each day's a blessing
And for some this might be true
But not knowing how your day will end
Makes it harder to get through

We know that we all have to die
And we accept that this is so
But when you're old you question
How long before I go?

We wonder will we have a stroke
Will we start to lose our minds
Will we end up in a nursing home
Being told that this is kind.

Old age is not for cowards
You need courage to see it through
Having folk around who love you
Makes it easier to do.

I must be thankful for what I have
To be ungrateful would be wrong
But if old age becomes a burden
Then I hope it doesn't last too long.

Hooked!

Here am I, caught like a fish
Trying to be free.
As I struggle
So all the more
The hook digs into me.

You threw the line
That captured me
What did I do to you?
Swimming aimlessly around
I had no need for you.

Innocent as was my way
I grabbed, I saw no hook
Now I end up captured
Another in your book.

It's too late now
To set me free
Now that I am caught
But I wish you'd fished
Another stream,
When looking for your sport.

Let them go

When children reach a certain age
They sometimes grow apart
Want to get away from home
And seek a fresh new start.

No need for parents anymore
That is the way some think
Ready now to take a chance
To swim or maybe sink.

If this is the way it seems to be
Don't keep them, let them go
In so doing you may find
A stronger bond may grow.

To parents suddenly faced with this
Do not see it as a fault
Be aware you've done your job
And independence taught.

Do not intrude let them feel free
Just watch the way you tread
And trust what you have taught them
Will stand them in good stead.

Only words

Words, words, words
Words of love you do impart
Falling gently from your lips
But are they coming
From your heart?

You tell me that you love me
And you seal it with a kiss
You say we have a special bond
That always will exist.

Words you speak mean nothing
So easily they come from you
It's your actions that will prove to me
If what you say is true.

My Daffodils

Slender, long
Their bodies green
Faces to the sun they raise
Trumpets gold
Acclaim the day
Let them stay…

Fluted edges
Stirred by the breeze
A golden carpet to be seen
Not long to live
Too short to gaze
Let them stay…

Don't shut them in,
Don't suffocate!
Leave them
In their natural state
Let them die
Their own way
Let them stay.

Candles

Some candles flicker
Then die out
Some give a gentle light
Others burn intensely
Making everywhere look bright.

Some people choose a gentle light
Where everything looks grey
The candle burning slowly
No brightness in their day.

There are those who choose to live
Their days all shining bright
Burning up their candles
Giving out their light.

The brightness that surrounds them
Is there so others see
Thinking not about themselves
They burn on merrily.

Slowly burn, the candle lasts
It's there for another day
Brightly shine the candles gone
And the day has flown away.

Don't complain!

You don't have many friends you say?
I wonder whose fault is that?
Maybe you're inclined to take
And give very little back.

It is good to choose friends carefully
And try to see who is true
But while you are busy looking
There are others looking at you.

They may find that you are difficult
Expect from them too much
See the sign that says to them
Don't come too close, don't touch.

Friends you could have many
I am certain this is true
But you have really got to change
It all depends on you.

Free Again!

I thought that this would happen
And I knew I was prepared
Let's call the wedding off we said,
I was glad, I didn't care.
We never meant the words
We spoke as we said 'Goodbye'.
We'd remain good friends
We both agreed, but knew it was a lie.
A life together was what we planned
But then it fell apart
We were ruled by our emotions
Thinking only with our hearts.
But once we saw the future
And realised how it would be
You saw that I was not for you,
And sadly you were not for me.
I wish you all the best my dear
And hope you'll find another
A woman who is subservient,
So you can feel above her.
A woman with no opinions
Who agrees to all your wishes
Loves to dust and clean all day
Is happy washing dishes.
I really tried to please you,
But I am sure that you could see
I was slowly going under,
Life was draining out of me.
Now I'm free to be myself
And I know there was a cost,
But it's better to have loved and lost
Than have you as 'My Boss'.

Believe

Do not look to find
Don't search to seek
Expect no answer
When you speak
HE is there, He hears.

Believe, do not question
Know what is true
Do more for others
Than they for you
HE is there, He sees.

Try to love, not to hate
Most are sinners
Few are saints
He watches patiently
And waits.

Never feel you walk alone
And no-one cares for you
HE is there
A constant friend
Watching over you.

Trust, hold out your hand
And give
This way you will receive
And great the rewards
That will come to you
You will feel as one
With Him.

You never know

Another year has now passed by
And Christmas is here once more
Memories stay and I relive
The childish dreams I had before
They were times when I was happy
We children never wanted much
We knew we had to be very good
Or Santa wouldn't call on us.

Our Xmas tree had coloured lights
They would glow and light the room
And we wanted them to stay forever
To take away the gloom.
So Xmas came around each year
We ate turkey and all the rest
Shared presents with the family
And dressed in our very best.

There was good will there was friendship
There was love that brought us close
And we thought that it would last forever
For we were young and full of hope.
Now I know there is no Santa Claus
I have accepted there are no elves
I realise those are magic dreams
For little boys and girls.

I'm older now and the magic's gone
And nothing is quite the same
But I think I will hang my stocking up
Just in case Santa calls again.

For Miriam's Eighteenth Birthday

I cannot send you gifts my dear
Cause I haven't any money
But these words that I am writing
Could make a dull day sunny.

I wish you every joy today
And a future that is bright
A home that gives security
And a bed to sleep at night.

The chance to see the good there is
And knowing you are loved
Forget the bad you know exists
Look at the stars that shine above.

It's not the presents you receive
Though nice I must confess
It's knowing people love you
That makes for happiness.

So look carefully around you
Count your blessings one by one
The years fly by and suddenly
You wonder where they've gone.

Some daughters never realize
And there are some who've never known
The love a mother had for them
Till they have children of their own.

Joyous!

I feel alive! I'm in love again,
Over the moon, and quite insane,
Take my hand come on and live
Make the most of what I give

Come fly with me enjoy the scene
Forget the past what might have been
Give yourself to life, to love
Search the heavens high above,
With lots of time we can explore
A million stars maybe even more

We will raise our voices sing out loud
Drift upon a soft white cloud
Soak our bodies in the rain
Then down to earth and back again,
Feeling great and quite insane,
I'm over the moon.
In love again.

The Play

The scene was set
The play was right
Not so long ago.
You produced the picture
I acted in the show.

The part I had
Was only small
That you had cast for me
It did not matter very much
It did not bother me.

So blindly I accepted
Joined you in the play
The fact it has not run long
No audience can blame.

Now the show has ended
My part no longer need
I will seek a new producer
And this time
I'll play the lead.

Save Something

Gone! Yes, it's gone
Truly gone.
So save the joy
Get out while there is time.

Let not decay set in,
Leave now
So memories gold
Lose not their shine.

Let not the light
That shone so bright grow dim,
Leaving nothing behind.

Protect those moments
Few given to enjoy
Go now whilst there is time.

Take heart.
The pain you feel will go
Leave now
Say goodbye,
Better be it so.

Thanks Dear Mum

Well dear Mum
We waved Goodbye
As I left for home,
I came to ease
The pain within.
I could not be alone.

It was a time I needed you,
And could not
Tell you why,
I knew you guessed
But you never asked
I was not forced to lie.

You've never been
A Mum who hugs,
Although I know you care
Soft, sweet words,
Not part of you
But you were always there.

Thanks dear Mum
For all you did
Being there helped
Me get through,

I'll always remember,
I will never forget
The special love
That came from you.

Conditioned?

I stare back at this monster no sign of life I see
But I can make it talk and sing if I choose that it should be.
I wonder should I let it talk should I withhold my power
Maybe make a cup of tea and have a nice quiet hour

Once awake it wont be quiet it gets inside my brain
And when I do my shopping I hear its voice again.
Confused I look and see the store, the one to choose I know,
The voice told me where to shop
And the store where I should go.

I'm now inside I see the shelves with so many different brands
I stop and wonder which to take and it's already in my hand.
From lane to lane my trolley's full so much for one alone
The check out girl gives me the bill
She does not hear me groan.

When I get home I'll pull its plug the monster then will die,
But could I be so callous I don't think I could try.
Conditioned, call it what you will alone and sad I'd be
I have no one to talk to no one visits me.

So give me all the soaps, the ads,
The films, the news, the weather,
Life alone without my telly,
Never... Never... Never!

I did my best

I was right, to say goodbye
For me and for you too
I could see the danger
Knew what I had to do.
I pushed aside the heartache
Found an inner strength
No more would we be lovers
Much better stay as friends.

I thought that you would help
Make it easier for me
You phone, so soon,
You say the words
"I need you, we must meet."

I hesitate what can I do
You know that I am weak
I tell myself "So what! Who cares?
Take what you can, and live."

So once more here I go again
It's sad and wrong, I know
For sure it would be over now
If you had never phoned.

Please don't shout

Hey! Wait a bit, don't give me that!
Who do you think you are shouting at?
Do you think the more you shout
You will lessen what it's all about?

Protestations spoken quietly
Offending not the way I hear
Will enable me to see quite clearly
If what you say is sincere.

But carry on, it matters not,
For when the storm subsides
I will see and know the truth
By looking in your eyes.

Lizzie and Manfred 1974

Look at us a happy pair
We have a little son
Bills and mortgage to be paid
It's only just begun.

These are the days so we are told
When love is all we need
It will help us through the bad times
And our worries will recede.

Hunger, bills and poverty
An overdraft that grows
Our characters will benefit
And true love then will show.

Our love is tested constantly
The troubles that we share
Make us both intolerant
When loving should be there.

To older folk who lived the same
And struggled this way too
Don't speak the usual platitudes
And tell us 'It's good for you'.

Look back, remember how you felt
When you were like us two
Then tell us in all honesty,
Was it good for you?

I am so sorry!

I just cannot help it
I know I was right
It was dirty and vermin
As are all mice.

I look at it sadly
And try to forget
Its neck crushed and broken
In the trap that I set.

Why should I bother?
It had to be done
Was it some mouse's mummy?
Was it some mouse's son?

I feel full of guilt
As I look at the trap
And see the poor mouse
With its poor broken neck.

I'm a coward I know
And honest must be
Next time a trap's set
It's not gonna be me.

Tell me now

If you are certain that you love me
Tell me now don't wait
Do not leave it for tomorrow
When tomorrow could be too late.

Tell me now while I am living
Do not wait till I am dead
Don't write your words of love on marble
When to me they should be said.

If you know you really love me
Waste not time but let me know
Do not leave me in the darkness
When your love could make me glow.

Death can call it gives no notice
No chance to speak unspoken vows
Let remorse not be your future
Say the words "I love you" now.

My Granddad

My Granddad's just died, I'm only a child
And I can't understand why
My Granddad's just died.
No visits no presents, not a word or a letter
The only reason they're here all together
Is that Granddad's just died.

Brothers and sisters not seen him in years
Now hugging each other and shedding their tears.
They bring beautiful flowers he can no longer see
I'm only a child and ask why should this be?

Now they speak of their past childhood days
When Granddad was young
And the games they had played
Of the times when they laughed
And the times when they cried
And protecting each other,
The times they had lied.

From this day on, they say they'll be friends
They will write and will visit, not lose touch again
It's sad when you think that Granddad's not here
He'd have loved all the chatter and seeing those dear.
I know how he waited for someone to call
A voice on the phone or a knock on his door

My Granddad has been buried
Tears and kind words have been said
I'm only a child and I can't understand
Why they waited till Granddad was dead.

Friendship

No words can say what is in my heart
When I think of you today,
You have been there when I have needed you
And what a difference you have made.

Always kind and caring
Putting up with my crazy ways
Listening to my tales of woe
Helping me through bad days.

Friends are special, they make you feel good
By their actions they show they care
But I'm sure there must have been many times
When you wished I would go elsewhere.

But then that's what friendship is all about
Not counting the cost not counting the time
Being there always not only when needed
Ready to listen to laugh and to smile.

So thank you for listening thanks for your time
Thank you for caring and being so kind
Thank you for taking the rough with the smooth
And thank you for being the person who's you.

Tolerance

Mother stands, the candles lit
The plaited bread is there,
On her head she wears a shawl
As she says her prayer.
'Blessed be the Lord our God'
Begins the prayer that's said,
Father takes and sips his wine,
'A blessing on your head'.

It is the eve of Sabbath,
And families around the world
Join together at this time,
Tomorrow, do no work.
This is a part of Jewish life,
Gone on for thousands of years,
Paid with scorn and ridicule
Paid with sweat and tears.

All of us are different,
Not one of us the same,
Many have their own Gods,
But choose a different name.
All think that they are special
Each thinks they know what's best,
Causing hate instead of loving
Doing harm to all the rest.

Remember we are all the same
Human, flesh and blood.
The best religion you can have
Is one which knows only love.

Please Go

My mind free of thought
Not thinking of what's past
Enjoying every moment
So I laugh.
Then you appear
Just long enough to cause me doubt
And question what is life all about
Always present, I am never free
For you are there a part of me
Quietly lurking behind the scene
You appear and torment me
The seeds of doubt that you have sown
Nurturing them you watch them grow
Too long you've been a part of me.
Go now guilt, and set me free.

Togetherness

There's nothing left for them to share
The love they had has gone
They live together but are apart
That's the way they get along.

They find comfort when they worry
In this they both can share
They enjoy and make the most of it
This way they think they care.

So, whenever there is trouble
Though small they make it big
It brings them closer for a while
And that's the way they live.

They must enjoy this way of life
For they play it out each day
What makes couples live like this?
Why choose to live this way?

Rock n' Roll

Here they are, just two kids
Having lots of fun
A night of 'Rocking round the clock'
They have only just begun.
Up in the air and over his head,
Swinging down through his legs,
Wearing all the Fifties gear
The swinging skirt, the slicked-back hair.

Now not so young so a little slow,
The music starts, and it's off they go
The bobby sox, no longer wear,
No pony tail, it's short cut hair,
The Cadillac has been and gone,
It's Mitsubishi from this day on
The slicked-back hair has now gone thin,
The body is no longer slim,
Coke is now replaced by beer,
But still ole Rock n' Roll is here.
Music of those carefree days,
Stars that shone, their names ablaze,
They may have gone, no more to see,
But they're alive, for you and me,
Good times they brought and hearts were light,
As we bee-bopped through the night.
The Fifties now have long since passed
But Rock n' Roll is here to last…
And last…and last…and last…

Memories of an East End Child
Violet Harrington

From a childhood in London's East End, lived in the Isle of Dogs, Violet Harrington traces an early life through the difficult times of the Blitz to becoming a fashion model. Often missing what seemed to be opportunities, she becomes a wife and mother.

Her engaging yet romantic story draws us into a variegated life that amply illustrates her childhood hardships during the second world war under bombardment and being bullied as a child. As it moves on through adult life we are presented with an empathetic glimpse into all the changes that happened in the world around her.

Her ideas of success often differed from her contemporaries' but her inspiring life, still an active thinker in her late 90s, is a lesson to us that true beauty lies within.

This book inspires us to live our lives to the full. Together with the companion book of her poems we discover this writer's talent for poetry and literature.

Hardcover: 978-3910667105

Paperback: 978-3910667099

Kindle and all e-book versions available

www.ingramcontent.com/pod-product-compliance
Lightning Source LLC
LaVergne TN
LVHW030411120526
838202LV00098BA/288